T0150420

WEATHER
FOR HILLWALKERS

WEATHER

FOR HILLWALKERS

MALCOLM THOMAS

The History Press

'I wish this book had been available when I first became interested in the weather half a century ago! ... I most certainly recommend it to anyone interested in understanding the weather and its effects on our outdoor pursuits.'

Bill Giles OBE
Senior Weatherman
BBC Weather Centre

Cover image: iatsun/iStock

This edition published 2019

First published 1995

The History Press
97 St George's Place, Cheltenham,
Gloucestershire, GL50 3QB
www.thehistorypress.co.uk

British Library Cataloguing in Publication Data.
A catalogue record for this book is available from the British Library.

ISBN 978 0 7509 9244 2

Typesetting and origination by The History Press
Printed and bound in Turkey by Imak

CONTENTS

ACKNOWLEDGEMENTS

I would like to thank the friends and colleagues who have made helpful suggestions during the writing of this book, in particular Rodney Blackall of the Met Office. I would also like to thank Mark Thomas for the incidental photographs, and Anne Reynolds for drawing the cloud sketches, and the following people who allowed me to use their cloud photographs: W.G. Pendleton/ G.A. Watt (Cirrus, p. 21); Mark Thomas (Cirrostratus, p. 22, Altocumulus, p. 25 and Stratus, p. 32); R.F. Saunders (Cirrocumulus, p. 23); R.W. Mason (Altostratus, p. 26 and Stratocumulus, p. 31); D.A. Warrilow (Nimbostratus, p. 27); Mark Thomas/J.H. Williams (Cumulus, p. 29); and N. Elkins (Cumulonimbus, p. 30).

Malcolm Thomas

FOREWORD TO THE FIRST EDITION

For years hillwalkers and climbers have wrestled with the fascinating but complex subject of mountain weather. Partly this has been due to a great void in the available literature between the embarrassingly simplistic and the confusingly complex. Malcolm Thomas has done his bit to fill this void with this excellent compromise.

It is perfectly aimed at the Mountain Leader Award syllabus and should put an end to hours of frustration and anguish for many a mountaineer. It will also act as an excellent springboard for those brave enough to launch into a search for a more in-depth understanding of the wondrous world of swirling mist, driving rain, waist-deep snow and crisp cloudless mornings – all the elements that make up our amazing mountain climate.

Nick Banks
Chief Instructor
National Mountain Centre, Plas y Brenin

FOREWORD

It's not an uncommon occurrence to look at a weather forecasting app to be told that it's 25 degrees and sunny, when in actual fact it's raining outside. The human world has fast moved into a technological age that has meant we tend not to trust our uninhibited observations of our natural environment. This is just one way in which we seem to have lost touch with nature as we have moved into a digital era, making the republication of *Weather for Hillwalkers* so very poignant at this time.

Slowly, the relationship between man and nature is healing as we begin to take responsibility for the damages we have done and attempt to reconnect. Republishing this book is a commentary on our endeavours to re-attune with the elements by reading the messages they send us and learning to interpret them. It is also a step to acknowledging our inherent bond with nature; a bond that cannot be replaced or feigned by technology.

No matter how advanced and accurate this technology might become, and no matter how dependent we may be on it, the weather will continue, as always, to prevail over the hills, mountains and beyond. Let this book be the starting point of understanding the natural world and learning to trust it again.

The Outdoor Guide and Julia Bradbury

PREFACE

There are a number of books available on the subject of weather, but these tend to be allied to interests and hobbies such as sailing and gardening. This book sets out to explain weather at a basic level and then to apply this knowledge to the mountain environment, with particular reference to the hills and mountains of the British Isles.

   The term weather describes the combination of a number of separate elements: wind, visibility, cloud, precipitation, temperature and so on. In this book each of the elements is looked at individually, and then the effects caused by hills and mountains are discussed and explained. In some cases there is a comfort factor: walking in persistent and heavy rain can be thoroughly uncomfortable and is a case in point. In other cases there is also a definite safety factor: strong winds over an exposed ridge, cloud lowering on to the hills reducing visibility, snowstorms and lightning are all potential hazards.

There can be very few people who have not seen a shower approaching, taken waterproofs from a rucksack and avoided a soaking. This is a simple example of using observation to forecast the weather in the short term, perhaps only five or ten minutes ahead. With a greater understanding, there are other signs that can be used to forecast the weather, on some occasions several hours ahead.

As we all know, professional forecasts are not always completely accurate and it is unlikely that they ever will be. However, a knowledge of weather can help in the interpretation of weather forecasts. For example, observation and understanding may indicate that the conditions will deteriorate earlier than the forecast suggested, or perhaps that precipitation is more likely to fall as snow than rain.

This book is suitable for anyone with an interest in hillwalking and climbing, and especially for students preparing for the Mountain Leader Award.

Malcolm Thomas

INTRODUCTION

There is something about the human instinct that will naturally take people up rather than down. When setting out for a walk in fine weather, either alone or with a group, there is a natural tendency to head towards the hills. Perhaps climbing upwards has something to do with lifting the spirit. Certainly the views are far more rewarding at the top of a mountain than at the bottom of a valley.

With increased leisure time, more people have had the satisfaction of hillwalking and climbing, and in turn have passed the interest on to a younger generation. Part of the pleasure of a day spent in the open air is observing the surroundings, whether it is watching a soaring bird of prey, noting the geology of a particular rock formation or perhaps taking note of the flora and fauna. There is always something to catch the eye.

The one factor that no one can fail to notice is the weather. It may be a point of interest, such as an

unusual cloud formation, or it could be something that affects comfort and perhaps safety. A day that started fine and then clouded over with heavy rain can be thoroughly miserable. Add strong winds and a lowering cloud base covering the hills, and the situation is then not only miserable but potentially dangerous as well.

The weather in the British Isles may not be as severe as in other parts of the world but there are occasions when it is barely survivable even for the best-equipped group. A mean windspeed of 95 knots gusting to 147 knots (nearly 170mph), has been recorded in the winter at the top of the Cairngorms, with the temperature 3°Celsius below freezing.

The part of the atmosphere in which weather occurs is really just a very thin envelope around the Earth. Even at its greatest depth, in the equatorial region, it is only in the order of 16 to 19km (10 to 12 miles) deep. Compared with the circumference of the Earth at around 40,225km (25,000 miles), this represents no more than the thickness of cigarette paper around a sphere the size of a football.

ONE

THE ATMOSPHERE

There are two distinct layers in the Earth's atmosphere; the lowest is the troposphere, with above it the stratosphere. The weather and nearly all clouds occur in the troposphere. The depth of the troposphere varies from about 16km (52,000ft) near the equator to around 8km (26,000ft) near the poles.

Temperature decreases with height at an average rate of 6.5 °C perkm or 2 °C per 1,000ft up to the top of the troposphere (the tropopause), and then becomes more or less constant with height in the stratosphere.

Air is a mixture of gases, comprising approximately by volume: nitrogen 78 per cent and oxygen 21 per cent, with the remaining 1 per cent being made up of trace gases including argon, carbon dioxide, neon, helium, krypton, ozone, methane, xenon and water vapour.

(Bigmouse108/iStock)

EXOSPHERE
>700 - 190 000 km

SPACECRAFT

MESOSPHERE
50 - 80 km

AURORA BOREALIS

METEORS

TROPOSPHERE
0 - 12 km

EXOBASE
>700 - 1000 km

THERMOSPHERE
80 - 700 km

KARMAN LINE
100 km

SATELLITES

STRATOSPHERE
12 - 50 km

OZONE LAYER
20 - 30 km

AIRPLANE

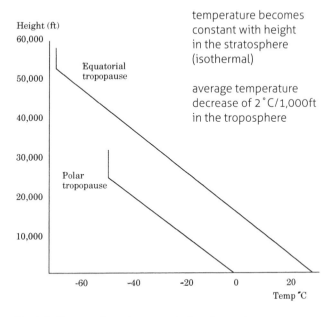

Fig. 1.1 Temperature decrease in the atmosphere.

WATER VAPOUR

Water vapour is essential for the formation of clouds and weather. It exists not only in a gaseous state, but also as a liquid (water) and as a solid (ice). The amount of water vapour present varies in time and space. Warm air can hold more water vapour than cold air. The amount of water vapour present in a volume of air at a given temperature can be expressed as a percentage of the maximum amount that the air can hold at that temperature, and is known as the relative humidity.

DEW POINT

Saturation of the air can occur in two ways: through cooling while the amount of water vapour remains constant, or through water vapour content increasing while the temperature remains constant. Either of these processes can be involved in the formation of cloud and fog, when the air becomes saturated and condensation occurs. The temperature at which air becomes saturated by cooling is known as the dew point.

LATENT HEAT

Latent heat is released when water vapour condenses into liquid (water). In fact latent heat is involved in all changes of state, i.e. from water vapour (gas) to water (liquid), and from water (liquid) to ice (solid). Condensation and freezing release heat; evaporation and melting require heat.

ATMOSPHERIC PRESSURE

The gases in the atmosphere have weight and therefore exert a pressure. Pressure can be measured in a number of ways using different units, but the most common method is to measure the pressure in millibars (mb) using an aneroid barometer. At sea level the average pressure is 1,013.25mb which equals 14.7lb/sq in. On a weather map the lines joining points of equal pressure are called isobars.

SOLAR ENERGY

The Sun emits short-wave radiation. Slightly more than half (51 per cent) of the amount intercepted by the atmosphere of the Earth reaches the ground. The rest is either reflected, absorbed by the various constituents of the atmosphere or 'back scattered'. The Earth re-radiates this energy in long-wave radiation, a small percentage of which goes directly into space, but most of it is involved in processes in the atmosphere before escaping to space.

The amount of solar radiation reaching the surface of the Earth varies for a number of reasons. Latitude is of major importance, *see* Fig. 1.2. Not only does less of the

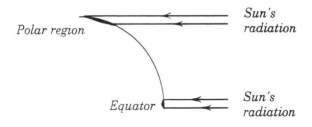

Fig. 1.2   Energy received is a maximum for unit area at the equator and a minimum at the poles.

Sun's energy reach the polar regions (none during the polar winter), but also more is reflected by the snow and ice cover. This results in a region of cold (sinking) air at the poles, and a region of warm (rising) air at the equator.

GENERAL CIRCULATION

Differential heating and movement of the air causes a circulation to be set up, as in Fig. 1.3. The warm rising air at the equator flows out towards the poles at high level, with a return flow from the poles towards the equator at low level. However, due to the Earth's rotation, the simple circulation becomes distorted, and results in the formation of three separate circulations, *see* Fig. 1.5.

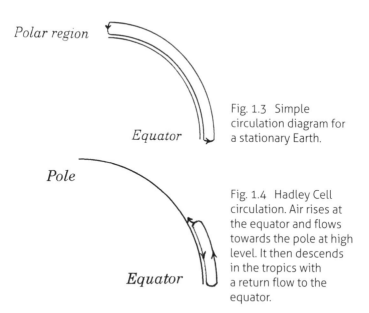

Fig. 1.3 Simple circulation diagram for a stationary Earth.

Fig. 1.4 Hadley Cell circulation. Air rises at the equator and flows towards the pole at high level. It then descends in the tropics with a return flow to the equator.

Suppose the air above the equator moves at the same speed as the Earth rotates. As it flows northwards at high level, its speed relative to the Earth will increase and its position in relation to the Earth will be deflected to the right. The result is a fast, high-level ribbon of air at around 30 degrees latitude, flowing from west to east. This is known as the subtropical jet stream.

   As more air arrives at high level from the equator, some of the air sinks back to the Earth's surface forming the high pressure desert regions of the world. From these high pressure areas there is an air flow not only

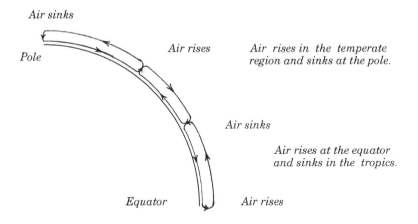

Fig. 1.5   Simplified global circulation.

towards the polar regions but also back towards the equator, establishing a circulation known as the Hadley cell, *see* Fig. 1.4. The air at the surface which is moving away from the tropical region towards the poles meets the cold dense polar air flowing towards the equator somewhere between 40 and 65 degrees latitude. The precise position varies not only from season to season but also from day to day and place to place, but it is in this region that the polar front becomes established when the warm tropical air is forced to rise over the cold dense polar air. The return high-level flow to the poles and the equator completes the simplified global circulation, *see* Fig. 1.5.

POLAR JET

In the region of the polar front, where the polar air and the subtropical air meet, another jet stream becomes established at around 30,000–35,000ft. It varies in strength and flows predominantly from west to east, at speeds on some occasions in excess of 200 knots. It is constantly changing in a waving oscillating pattern. The whole pattern tends to progress from west to east around the pole, with the result that the British Isles can be either in the warmer subtropical air or the colder polar air, or in the transitional stage. These global oscillations are known as Rossby Waves.

Fig. 1.6 shows the British Isles in the warmer subtropical air, with the jet stream to the north of the country. In Fig 1.7 the pattern has moved south-eastwards and much of the British Isles is now moving into the polar air, with the jet stream across the south of the country. It is this movement of the upper air pattern that causes the change from warm to cooler air across the UK.

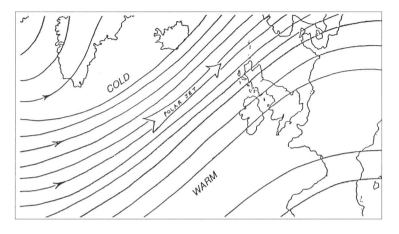

Fig. 1.6 Upper air chart at 300mb (30,000ft). The lines shown are contour lines at constant pressure level.

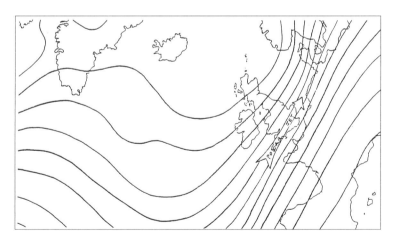

Fig. 1.7 Upper air chart at 300mb (30,000ft). The lines shown are contour lines at constant pressure level.

TWO

CLOUDS AND CLOUD FORMATION

Before we can proceed it is necessary to look at cloud types and formation, and the heights at which clouds form. Recognition of clouds and an understanding of how they are formed is essential if observation is to be used as a method of short-term forecasting.

The original classification of clouds was conceived by the pharmacist Luke Howard in the early nineteenth century. The Latin names he gave them are still in use today. There are basically only four names, although in some cases the names are combined to give a better description of the cloud. The term 'alto' was introduced to indicate high cloud (as in the music terminology), but in fact is now usually used to indicate medium-level cloud.

The four types and their meanings are: **Cirrus**, a tuft or filament (as in hair); **Stratus**, a layer; **Cumulus**, a pile or heap; and **Nimbus**, rain bearing.

Recognition of clouds is not always easy. Cloud structures can change very quickly, and judging their height is something that only comes with experience. It is usual to categorise clouds as low, medium and high, and with knowledge of cloud structure this does help identification.

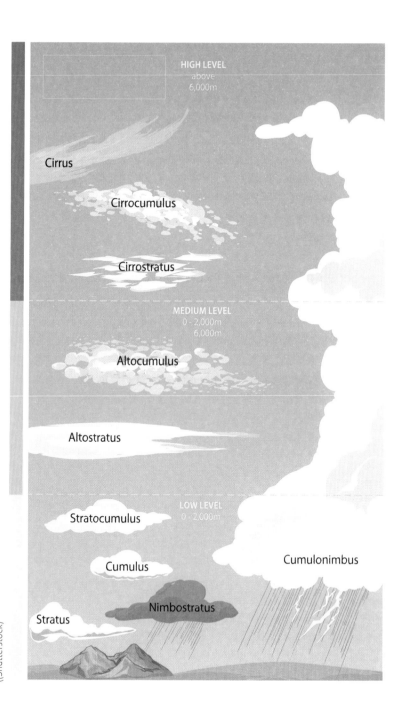

HIGH LEVEL
above
6,000m

Cirrus

Cirrocumulus

Cirrostratus

MEDIUM LEVEL
0 - 2,000m
6,000m

Altocumulus

Altostratus

LOW LEVEL
0 - 2,000m

Stratocumulus

Cumulus

Cumulonimbus

Nimbostratus

Stratus

((Shutterstock))

HIGH CLOUDS

Cirrus occurs either in wisps or filaments, sometimes called mares' tails, or it can form into quite thick 'sheaves'.

Cirrus clouds form between 18,000 and 30,000ft, the lower base being in the polar air and the higher base in the warm tropical air.

Cirrostratus is a thick layer of cirrus, often completely covering the sky. It is through cirrostratus that a ring can sometimes be seen around the Sun or Moon; this is due to refraction through the ice crystals.

Cirrocumulus is cirrus with very small crenellations (blobs). This results in a picturesque sky, particularly at sunset but is seen fairly infrequently.

Height in ft

30,000

25,000

20,000

15,000

Fig. 2.1   Cirrus.

Fig. 2.2   Cirrus in wisps or filaments.

Fig. 2.3   Cirrus in dense patches.

Height in ft

Fig. 2.4 Cirrostratus.

Fig. 2.5 A veil of cirrostratus covering the sky, with patches of altocumulus underneath, increasing in the distance.

Height in ft

Fig. 2.6   Cirrocumulus.

Fig. 2.7   Cirrocumulus (cirrus in small blobs).

MEDIUM CLOUDS

Medium-level clouds generally form between around 8,000 and 18,000ft, although in the case of nimbostratus the base often lowers to well below 8,000ft.

Altocumulus is a layer of cloud with large elements (blobs). It can be quite thin, allowing plenty of sunlight through, or in a thick layer, completely shutting out the Sun.

Altostratus is a uniform layer of cloud with little detail. It can sometimes look like cirrostratus if it is fairly thin. The Sun or Moon often appears as though looked at through ground glass.

Fig. 2.8   Altocumulus.

Nimbostratus is a flat featureless cloud, which is thick enough to produce rain. It is formed as altostratus lowers and thickens.

Fig. 2.9   Altocumulus in a thin layer.

Fig. 2.10   Altocumulus in a thick layer, shutting out the Sun.

Height in ft

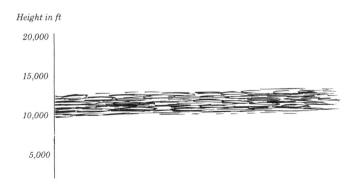

Fig. 2.11   Altostratus.

Fig. 2.12   A layer of altostratus through which the Sun can just be seen.

Height in ft

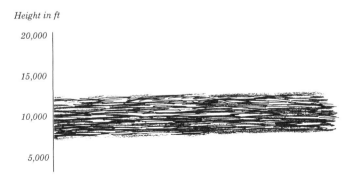

Fig. 2.13   Nimbostratus.

Fig. 2.14   Nimbostratus in a thick, featureless layer, with patches of stratus below, in the valley.

LOW CLOUDS

Cumulus gives the appearance of pieces of cotton wool drifting across the sky. As further development takes place, the tops start to look more like cauliflowers. Cumulus of sufficient depth can produce showers.

The base of cumulus is generally between 2,000 and 3,000ft. In cold polar air in the winter, and in very moist air, it can be lower, between 1,000 and 1,500ft, while in warmer tropical air in the summer the base often lies between 4,000 and 5,000ft.

Height in ft

Fig. 2.15 Cumulus.

Fig. 2.16   Patches of shallow cumulus.

Fig. 2.17   Cumulus with strong vertical development.

Cumulonimbus clouds are formed from the development of cumulus clouds as they increase in depth. The tops can extend to over 30,000ft, producing severe thunderstorms.

For clouds to be classified as cumulonimbus, the tops must start to take on a fibrous appearance. It can be just slightly fibrous as the ice crystals start to form, or the more classic 'anvil' shape as the tops spread out.

The base of cumulonimbus is similar to cumulus in that it is generally between 2,000 and 3,000ft. In cold polar air it tends to be slightly lower and in warm tropical air in the summer it can rise to nearer 5,000ft.

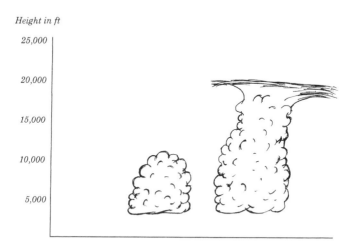

Fig. 2.18 Cumulus developing into cumulonimbus.

Fig. 2.19 Cumulonimbus with the tops just starting to become fibrous.

Fig. 2.20 Well-developed cumulonimbus with the fibrous tops spread out.

Stratocumulus is a layer of cloud with a uniform base. It can either be a continuous sheet, but more often has some breaks. The base of stratocumulus can be anywhere between 1,500 and 7,000ft. It is similar in appearance to altocumulus, particularly when the base is fairly high.

Stratus can either be in a continuous sheet with a grey, featureless base, or in ragged shreds, which is known as fractostratus. The base of stratus can be anywhere between the surface and around 2,000ft.

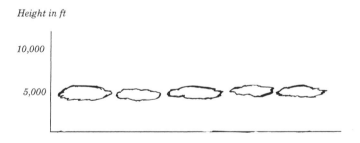

Fig. 2.21 Stratocumulus.

Fig. 2.22   A continuous fairly thick layer of stratocumulus.

Height in ft

5,000

Fig. 2.23   Stratus.

Fig. 2.24 Stratus in a continuous layer.

Fig. 2.25 Stratus in ragged shreds.

CLOUD FORMATION

Clouds are formed in two ways: firstly, air can be cooled to the point where it becomes saturated, or secondly, the air can pick up moisture as it flows over the sea or ocean. In both cases the point is reached when the air can hold no more moisture in the form of water vapour. Condensation then occurs, forming tiny water droplets, or if it is sufficiently cold, ice crystals. Cooling is more common, and can occur either when the air is forced to rise, or to a lesser extent, by mixing because of turbulence.

The first and perhaps most obvious example of cooling through forced ascent is the formation of cumulus during the day through convective heating. The Sun's radiation warms the Earth, and pockets of air rise in thermals, cooling as they expand until condensation takes place, causing tiny water droplets to form into a cloud.

The second example, familiar to anyone used to walking in the mountains, is when air is forced to rise over high ground. Cooling and the formation of cloud takes place with the cloud frequently covering the tops of the hills.

Height in ft

Fig. 2.26 Formation of cumulus through convective heating.

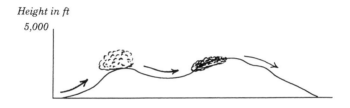

Fig. 2.27 Formation of cumulus or stratus as air is forced to rise over the hills.

The third example is cooling by mass ascent over a much larger area. The previous examples were of cloud formed locally with strong uplift, perhaps just covering a range of hills. In the case of mass ascent associated with a weather front, the air rises much more slowly over hundreds of miles, forming extensive layers of cloud.

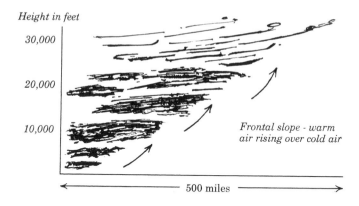

Fig. 2.28   Cooling by mass ascent to form extensive layers of cloud.

THREE

AIR MASSES

The term air mass is used to describe a large flow of air with similar characteristics in terms of temperature and humidity. Consequently, it also has similarities in terms of cloud types and also clarity and visibility. Air masses are identified in terms of their source of origin and their modifying land or sea influence, for example tropical maritime or polar continental.

In chapter 1 (*see* Figs 1.6 and 1.7), we saw how the position of the polar jet determined whether the British Isles were in the cold polar air or the warmer tropical air. Due to the geographical position of the country there are other factors that can influence and modify the flow from either direction. The large expanse of the Atlantic Ocean to the west tends to add moisture to the flow, whereas the flow from the east or south-east from the continent is normally drier. There are six distinct air masses that affect the British Isles, four of which are from a cold source and two from a warm source.

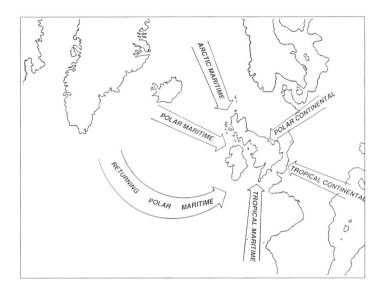

Fig. 3.1   Air masses affecting the British Isles in terms of source and modifying influence.

The cold air masses are polar maritime, returning polar maritime, Arctic maritime and polar continental. The two warm air masses are tropical continental and tropical maritime.

POLAR MARITIME

Polar maritime is the most common type of air mass affecting the British Isles. Its source is the Greenland or Canadian Arctic area. As the cold air moves southwards it is warmed from below by the comparatively warm ocean. Warming has the effect of forcing air to rise in convective currents, inducing the formation of cumulus clouds or, if the convection is sufficiently strong, cumulonimbus. The weather characteristics associated with a polar maritime air mass are as follows:

Visibility: Excellent with a 'sparkling' clarity to the air.
Winds: Predominantly from a west to north-west direction and often quite blustery in association with any showers.
Weather: In the winter and early spring, convection is set off over the sea. The western side of the British Isles experiences frequent showers, affecting the Welsh mountains, the Lake District and the western mountains of Scotland. Due to the low freezing level of the air, the showers frequently fall as snow over the high ground. In late spring and summer, the convection tends to be initiated by the warmer land, and showers are likely to fall over the whole of the country. With sufficient depth of convection, thunderstorms are

not uncommon, tending to pass quickly in the north-westerly flow.

POINTS TO NOTE

1   Cloud base is normally between 1,500 and 2,500ft above sea level, intermittently covering the high ground.

2   Snow showers can arrive quite suddenly, producing white-out conditions.

3   Early morning in the late spring and summer can be deceptive in that there is often little or no cloud at first. The cloud is produced by convection during the day as the land becomes warmer, resulting in showers, and the cloud intermittently covering the hills by mid-morning and in the afternoon.

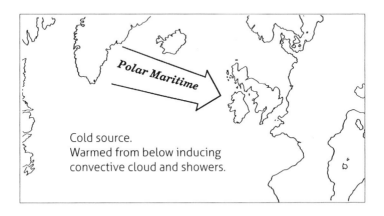

Fig. 3.2

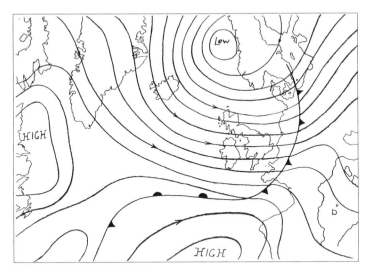

Fig. 3.3 Weather chart showing a polar maritime air mass over the British Isles. Note the low pressure to the north, and high pressure to the south-west of the British Isles, with a run of isobars from a north-westerly direction over the country.

RETURNING POLAR MARITIME

Returning polar maritime has an original cold source similar to polar maritime, but it becomes modified by the long sea track. In effect, the air travels southwards over the Atlantic Ocean before turning north-eastwards over the British Isles. It becomes warmer and moister in the lower layers, although the colder air at higher level is retained. In some respects the characteristics are similar to a polar maritime air mass, but the extra moisture at low level does have implications for cloud formation and possibly fog, especially on the western side of the British Isles. The weather characteristics associated with a returning polar maritime air mass are as follows:

Visibility: Generally good.
Winds: Predominantly south-westerly of varying strength.
Weather: Extensive cumulus cloud, often producing showers anywhere over the British Isles. In addition, the western side of the country can be subject to low stratus cloud and patchy fog because of the extra moisture at low level. Further inland, particularly in the lee of any high ground, the stratus tends to lift and dissipate.

1   Cloud base is normally around 2,000 to 2,500ft above sea level, intermittently covering the high ground. Also, patchy cloud with the base between the surface and 1,000ft on western-facing hills and coasts, becoming quite extensive on some occasions.

2   Hill and coastal fog can be a particular problem on the western side of the country. The Grampians and the Peak District towards the eastern side experience better conditions, with the cloud bases slightly higher and more broken.

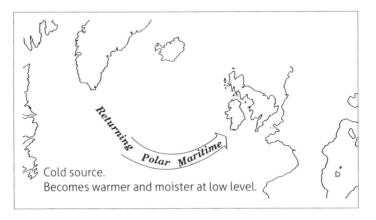

Fig. 3.4

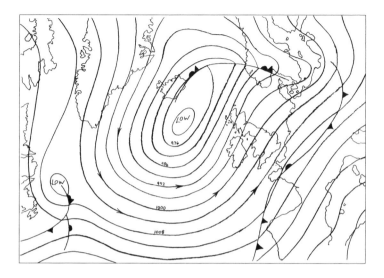

Fig. 3.5 Weather chart showing a returning polar maritime
air mass over the British Isles. Note the low pressure to
the north-west of the British Isles with the flow moving
southwards from Greenland before turning towards the east
north-east over the British Isles.

ARCTIC MARITIME

The Arctic maritime air mass has similar characteristics to the polar maritime but has an even colder source. On some occasions, depressions form in the northerly flow bringing organised areas of snow southwards, with the Scottish mountains experiencing the worst of the conditions. Weather characteristics associated with an Arctic maritime air mass are as follows:

Visibility: Excellent, virtually unlimited.
Winds: Northerly, often strong to gale force.
Weather: Arctic maritime is a winter feature and it brings some of the severest weather to the mountainous regions of the British Isles, especially the Scottish mountains. Frequent and heavy snow showers are common, not only over the high ground but also anywhere exposed to the northerly flow. It is normally an Arctic maritime flow that brings snow showers to East Anglia and Kent, with the flow off the North Sea.

POINTS TO NOTE

1   Cloud base is normally around 1,000 to 2,000ft above sea level, intermittently covering the high ground.

2   Freezing level is typically between 500 and 1,000ft, giving sub-zero temperatures even at low level.

3   Winds are often of gale force with resulting high chill factor (*see* chapter 6, Fig. 6.3).

4   Snow showers over the Scottish mountains, especially the Grampians, often merge together to give almost continuous heavy snow with white-out conditions.

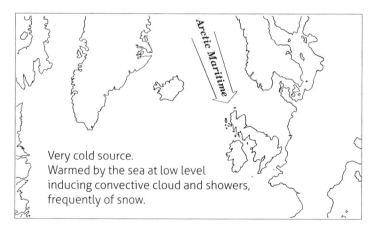

Fig. 3.6

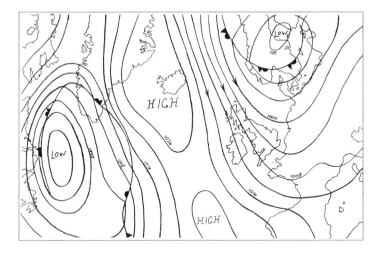

Fig. 3.7 Weather chart showing an Arctic maritime air mass over the British Isles. Note the low pressure over Scandinavia, and high pressure over Iceland and eastern Greenland. The result is a northerly run of isobars over the British Isles. The pressure differential between the areas of low and high pressure is often sufficient to produce gale force winds over the northern part of the country.

POLAR CONTINENTAL

A polar continental air mass derives from the cold, dry source of Scandinavia or Russia, although the short sea track over the North Sea adds moisture to the lower levels. As the continent warms up during the summer, the source becomes warmer, but the air remains essentially dry. The weather characteristics associated with a polar continental air mass are as follows:

Visibility: Generally fairly good in an easterly flow, but if the flow veers slightly to the south-east, the tendency is to pick up more pollution from industrial sources, causing rather hazy conditions. A polar continental flow often persists for several days with the visibility becoming increasingly hazy.

Winds: A cold easterly in the winter of varying strength. The dryness of the air (low dew point) increases the chill factor (*see* chapter 6).

Weather: The increase of low-level moisture from the North Sea often results in a layer of cloud on the eastern side of the country. This can be thick enough to give light snow flurries over the Yorkshire Moors and the eastern side of the Grampians in the winter. The western side of the country can have virtually cloud-free conditions.

1   A polar continental flow is normally associated with a persistent area of high pressure over Scandinavia and the north of Scotland, and can last for several days. It provides good, if somewhat hazy, conditions for walking and climbing anywhere on the western side of the country, particularly in the Western Highlands and Western Isles. It tends to be most common in early winter and May.

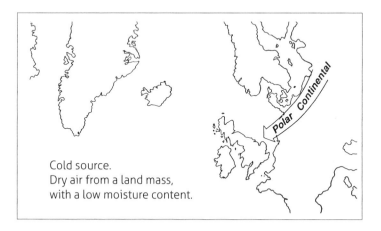

Cold source.
Dry air from a land mass,
with a low moisture content.

Polar Continental

Fig. 3.8

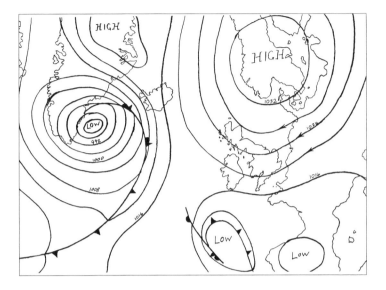

Fig. 3.9 Weather chart showing a polar continental air mass over the British Isles. Note the high pressure over Scandinavia with an east to south-easterly flow over the British Isles.

TROPICAL CONTINENTAL

This is a summer feature, with the flow from a south or south-easterly direction. With its origins over the Sahara Desert, the flow is essentially very dry and warm, although moisture at high levels and high temperatures can lead to severe thunderstorms. The weather characteristics associated with a tropical continental air mass are as follows:

Visibility: Tends to be rather hazy, especially in the morning, and often with a 'milky' look to the sky caused by dust particles in suspension.

Winds: Generally light from the south-east quarter, although often with a sea breeze near the coast.

Weather: Hot and sunny, producing the highest temperatures of the summer. A fine spell frequently ends with an area of thunderstorms moving northwards across the country.

POINTS TO NOTE

1   Fine conditions in the mountains, although rather hazy, and it can be very dehydrating.

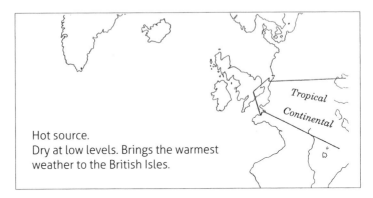

Hot source.
Dry at low levels. Brings the warmest weather to the British Isles.

Fig. 3.10

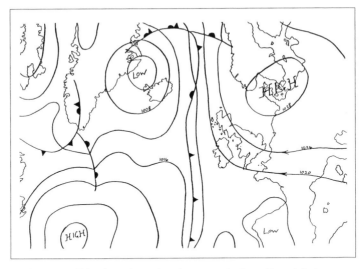

Fig. 3.11 Weather chart showing a tropical continental air mass over the British Isles. Note the area of high pressure (anticyclone) to the east of the British Isles with a south to south-easterly flow over the country.

TROPICAL MARITIME

This is a frequent air mass over the country, equally common in winter and summer, bringing warm, moist air with origins in the subtropical region. Moisture in the lower layers leads to extensive low cloud over south-west-facing coasts and hills. Further inland the cloud tends to lift and break, especially in the summer, and to the lee of high ground. Weather characteristics associated with a tropical maritime air mass are as follows:

Visibility: Often fairly poor with mist and fog around the coasts, especially in winter and springtime when the sea is comparatively cold.
Winds: Mainly south-westerly in direction and of varying strength.
Weather: Extensive low cloud often gives fog and persistent drizzle on the western side of the British Isles.

POINTS TO NOTE

1   Freezing level is normally above all the mountains in the British Isles in the winter.

2   The cloud will often lift and break inland in the spring and summer, making the Peak District, the Yorkshire Moors and the Grampians the more favoured areas of high ground in the British Isles.

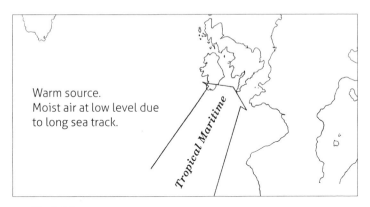

Warm source.
Moist air at low level due
to long sea track.

Tropical Maritime

Fig. 3.12

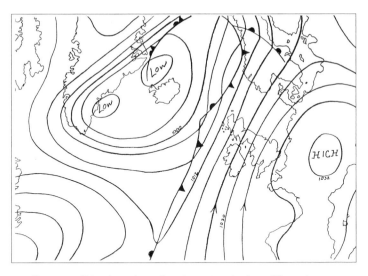

Fig. 3.13 Weather chart showing a tropical maritime air mass over the British Isles. Note the polar front lying to the north of the UK, high pressure over Europe, and a run of isobars from a south-westerly direction across the British Isles.

FOUR

FRONTS AND DEPRESSIONS

So far we have looked at airstreams affecting the British Isles that have similar characteristics (homogenous). Severe weather in terms of persistent, heavy rain and snow is normally associated with depressions and frontal systems. The concept of fronts was put forward in the 1920s by Norwegian meteorologists. They realised that there was often a sharp dividing line between the warm and cold air, with extensive cloud along the division. The term front was derived from the First World War expression denoting the division between opposing forces.

Where cold polar air meets warmer subtropical air, the tendency is for the cold dense air to undercut the warm less-dense air, forcing it to rise. The result is cooling, condensation and the formation of cloud and weather. The activity on a front in terms of the amount of precipitation depends largely on the temperature contrast. Fronts can vary from just a line of cloud with

STANDARD NOTATION OF FRONTS

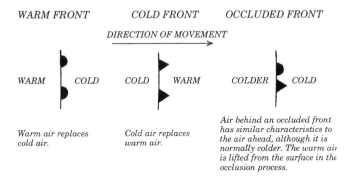

Fig. 4.1   Standard notation of fronts.

little depth, to a mass of cloud producing persistent heavy rain.

If we examine an almost stationary ('quasi-stationary') polar front over the Atlantic, with polar air to the north and warmer subtropical air to the south, it can exist in a state of balance, *see* Fig. 4.2. Small waves often run along the front in the flow, but they are hardly noticed and do not develop; these are known as stable waves, *see* Fig. 4.3. A good analogy is the ripple that runs along the length of a rope when you flick the end of it.

If, however, the pressure at the tip of the wave continues to fall a depression forms, known as an open wave depression, *see* Fig. 4.4. The polar front

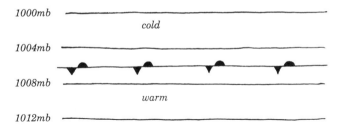

Fig. 4.2   A polar front in a state of balance (quasi-stationary).

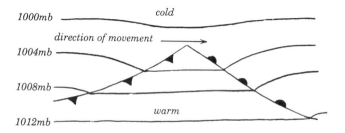

Fig. 4.3   A stable frontal wave. A slight fall of pressure occurs at the wave tip but does not deepen significantly.

becomes increasingly distorted, with distinct warm and cold fronts being formed. The warm tropical air (the warm sector) lies between the two. The direction of movement is normally parallel to the isobars in the warm sector. An open wave depression continues to deepen in the developing stage, which lasts typically for about 48 hours. During this time the cold front moves slightly faster than the warm front, eventually

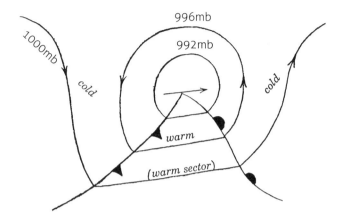

Fig. 4.4   Open wave depression.

catching it up, *see* Fig. 4.6. The result of this is that the warm air in the warm sector is lifted off the surface to form an occluded front, *see* Fig. 4.12.

The depression will continue to deepen after the start of the occlusion process, generally for about 18 hours, after which the decaying process begins. The movement becomes slower as it starts to fill (the pressure rises), and the tendency is to turn to the left and finally become stationary.

The clouds associated with a frontal system can extend several hundred miles ahead of the surface front and have a characteristic structure which is fairly easily recognized. On a weather chart a warm front is

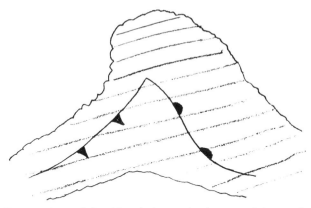

Fig. 4.5   Area of cloud in relation to the fronts and depression.

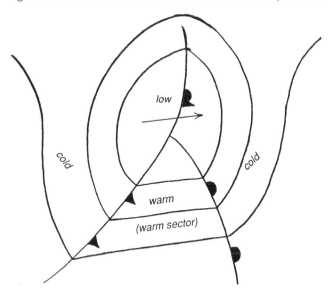

Fig. 4.6   The start of the occlusion process as the cold front catches up the warm front.

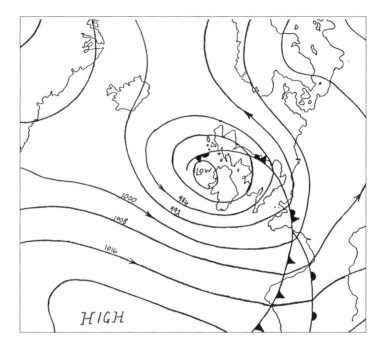

Fig. 4.7 The chart shows a fully occluded, stationary depression to the north-west of Ireland, with the associated occluded front from the Western Isles along the eastern side of England to the Brest peninsula in France.

denoted as a single line, but that only marks its position at the Earth's surface. The division between the cold air ahead and the warm air behind is a forward-sloping rather than vertical separation. In fact the slope is very shallow, typically at a gradient of 1 in 150 (or 1 mile in the vertical for 150 miles in the horizontal). As the

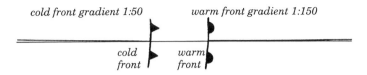

Fig. 4.8   Cold front and warm front gradients.

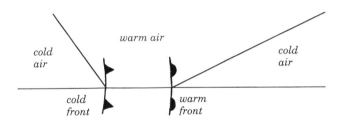

Fig. 4.9   Exaggerated slope for diagrammatic purposes.

first cloud associated with the front is generally 4 miles high (20,000–25,000ft), it is possible to detect an approaching front 500 to 600 miles away. For example, the high cirrus cloud of a warm front could be over eastern England when the surface front approaching from the west was near the west coast of Ireland.

In contrast, the slope on a cold front is backward-sloping, at a gradient of about 1 in 50, as the cold air undercuts the warm air. The true gradient of a cross-section through a warm and cold front would be represented as in Fig. 4.8. On this scale it is barely detectable as a gradient at all. For diagrammatic

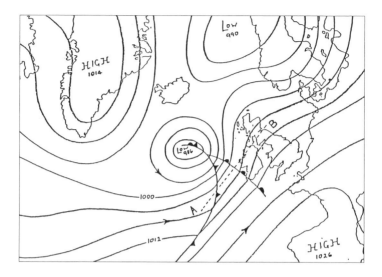

Fig. 4.10 An occluding frontal system approaching the British Isles.

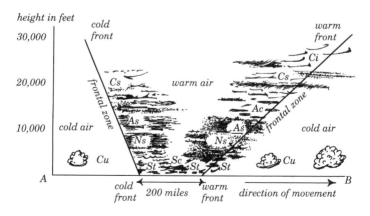

Fig. 4.11 Cross-section of cloud structure at A–B.

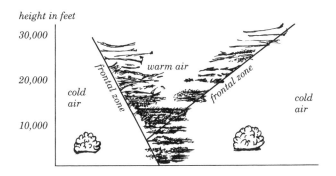

Fig. 4.12   Cross-section through an occluded front.

Ci	–	Cirrus
Cs	–	Cirrostratus
Ac	–	Altocumulus
As	–	Altostratus
Ns	–	Nimbostratus
Sc	–	Stratocumulus
St	–	Stratus
Cu	–	Cumulus

purposes it is common to exaggerate the slope to illustrate the cloud structure and the associated weather.

The cloud formation of approaching fronts is perhaps the most easily recognisable sequence. In view of the associated adverse weather in terms of rain and snow, strong winds and low cloud, it is worth becoming familiar with the cloud structure of a frontal system. Fig. 4.10 shows a system approaching the British Isles from the west, with the occlusion process started. The line

A–B represents a cross-section through the warm and cold fronts. Fig. 4.11 shows the cloud structure at the line A–B. Fig. 4.12 shows a cross-section through the occluded front where the warm air has been lifted off the surface.

Occasionally, cumulonimbus cloud is mixed with the layered cloud on a cold front, with the possibility of a thunderstorm occurring as the cold front passes through.

FIVE

WINDS

No two frontal systems are ever quite the same in terms of cloud formation and associated weather. Sometimes there are just layers of cloud with little or no precipitation, while at other times a system can bring extensive rain, or in winter snow, right across the British Isles. The fact that a front is approaching should be a warning of potentially adverse weather in terms of lowering cloud base, precipitation and usually strengthening winds. There is, however, no way of knowing simply from cloud observation how active a frontal system is going to be. One element that should be observed is the wind, both in terms of its strength and direction. Wind can sometimes give a clue as to how active a system will be, but perhaps more importantly its direction can suggest whether precipitation in winter will fall as rain or snow.

Wind results from the pressure difference between two regions, causing air to flow from high to low

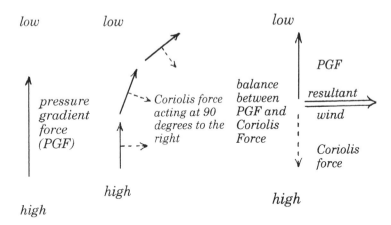

Left: Fig. 5.1   Pressure gradient force causes air to flow from high pressure to low.
Centre: Fig. 5.2   The action of the Coriolis force.
Right: Fig. 5.3   Balance between the Coriolis force and the pressure gradient force.

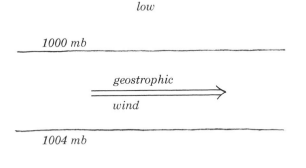

Fig. 5.4   The geostrophic wind.

pressure, *see* Fig. 5.1. However, once air starts to move it becomes subject to the Coriolis force, which arises from the Earth's rotation and acts at 90 degrees to the direction of the air flow. This force causes a deflection to the right in the northern hemisphere and to the left in the southern hemisphere, *see* Fig. 5.2. The deflection continues until a balance is reached between the Coriolis Force and the pressure gradient force, *see* Fig. 5.3.

The resultant wind, called the geostrophic wind, blows parallel to the isobars (lines of equal pressure), as illustrated in Fig. 5.4. It represents the free flow of air, generally taken to be at around 2,000ft, although the level varies depending on the air mass and the time of day. From Fig. 5.4 it can be seen that for an observer with their back to the wind, the low pressure will be on the left and the high pressure will be on the right. This is Buys Ballot's law, and is an important law of meteorology.

Taking the principle a step further, it follows that if the low pressure is always on the left, the air flow will be anti-clockwise around an area of low pressure, and clockwise around an area of high pressure, *see* Fig. 5.5.

Another factor to be taken into account when considering the wind at surface level is friction. This varies depending on the roughness of the terrain and the time of day, and has two effects. The first is a reduction in geostrophic wind speed, generally to between a half

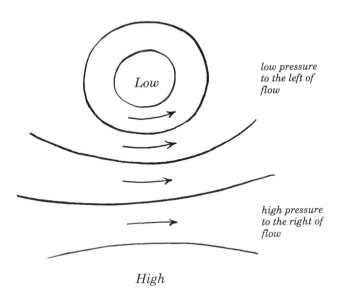

*low pressure
to the left of
flow*

*high pressure
to the right of
flow*

Fig. 5.5   Direction of air flow around depressions (low pressure areas) and anticyclones (high pressure areas).

and two-thirds. Secondly, the reduction in speed upsets the balance between the pressure gradient force and the Coriolis force, and results in the direction 'backing' by around 30 degrees, *see* Figs 5.6 and 5.6(a). The result is that the surface wind blows into the low pressure area and out from the high pressure area, *see* Fig. 5.7.

It might appear illogical that with air flowing in towards the centre of a depression that the pressure continues to fall, or rather that as more air flows into

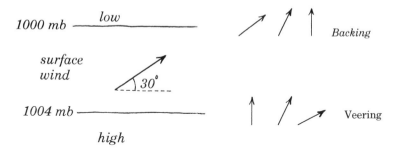

Fig. 5.6   Backing as a result of the balance between the pressure gradient force and the Coriolis force being upset.

Fig. 5.6(a)   Backing and veering. Backing is an anti-clockwise directional wind change. Veering is a clockwise directional wind change.

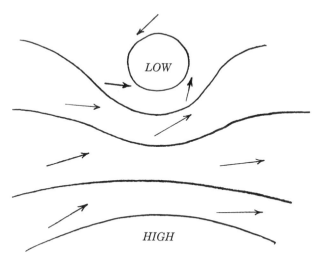

Fig. 5.7   The wind blows into the low pressure area and out from the high pressure area.

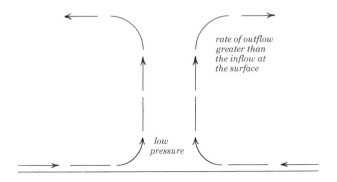

rate of outflow greater than the inflow at the surface

low pressure

Fig. 5.8   Air flowing into a depression at the surface, rising through the depression, and flowing out at high level. As long as the outflow remains greater than the inflow, the depression will continue to deepen.

the centre that the pressure does not rise. The point to remember is that when air flows into and up through a depression the outflow at high level is greater than the inflow at the surface, *see* Fig. 5.8. Until the rate of outflow decreases to less than the inflow at the base, the depression will continue to deepen.

With a knowledge of depressions and fronts, it is now possible to look at the effects of the track of a depression crossing the British Isles from the west on the wind directions and on precipitation.

In Fig. 5.9 a winter depression is shown crossing the British Isles, with its centre to the north of Scotland.

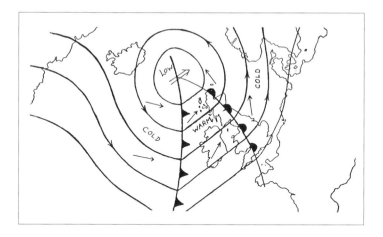

Fig. 5.9 A frontal system crossing the British Isles with the centre of the depression to the north of Scotland. The winds over the country are south to south-westerly before veering north-westerly behind the cold front.

Remembering where the warm and cold air areas associated with the system are located, we would expect the precipitation over the country to fall as rain rather than snow. The wind direction would be predominantly from the south-west, veering to north-westerly after the passage of the cold front.

In Fig. 5.10 the depression is taking a more southerly track across Scotland. In this case the precipitation would fall predominantly as rain to the south in the warmer air, but over much of Scotland would fall as snow in the colder air. Note the wind direction over the

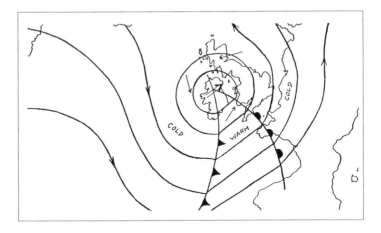

Fig. 5.10 On this chart the centre of the depression is further south, crossing Northern Ireland and the Lake District. The winds over Scotland are backing to an easterly direction as the depression approaches.

Highlands of Scotland as the depression approaches. It backs from southerly to easterly ahead of the depression, continuing to back through northerly to north-westerly as the depression moves across the country. Over the Welsh mountains, precipitation starts as snow ahead of the warm front, but turns to rain as the warm front approaches from the west. The wind remains from a south to south-westerly direction.

Points to note are that with a depression approaching from the west, winds will normally strengthen and back.

If the winds back round to an easterly direction, the centre of the depression is likely to pass close to, or to the south of, the observer. In this case precipitation is likely to be prolonged. In any case the precipitation is likely to fall as snow in the winter, particularly over higher ground. Strong winds associated with a deep and vigorous depression may produce blizzard conditions.

One other point worth noting is that in the cold air ahead of a warm front in the winter, precipitation can sometimes start as snow, particularly over the high ground, and then turn to rain as the warm front and the warmer air arrives from the west.

SIX

WEATHER IN THE MOUNTAINS

In general, it is colder, wetter and windier in the mountains. So far we have looked at the weather in broad terms but it is now necessary to consider how the various elements are affected by the high ground.

TEMPERATURE

The rate at which temperature decreases with height – the lapse rate – varies depending on the air mass. For example, it can be around 3˚C/1,000ft between the surface and 3,000ft on occasions, but the average figure of 2˚C/1,000ft provides a general rule of thumb calculation. On that basis, simple arithmetic turns a temperature of 6˚C at low level into sub-zero values high up on many British mountains.

Another consideration with regard to temperature is the chill factor, *see* page 64.

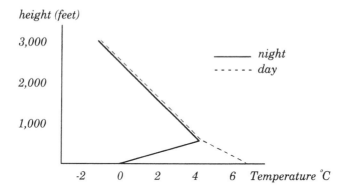

Fig. 6.1   A typical lapse rate profile of a temperature inversion.

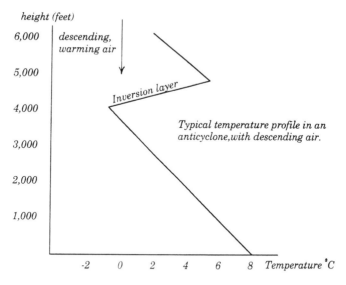

Fig. 6.2   Typical temperature profile in an anticyclone, with descending air.

TEMPERATURE INVERSION

A temperature increase with height, is known as an inversion, and can occur over shallow layers in the atmosphere. Fig. 6.1 shows a typical profile of the lapse rate just before dawn on a clear night with little or no wind. The ground cools by radiation, and then conduction cools the air close to the ground. The cooling spreads upwards, but only through a shallow layer. In this situation the temperature in a valley will be lower than the surrounding hills. After dawn, the Sun's radiation warms the ground, which in turn warms the air near it. Convection spreads the warmth upwards. The inversion layer quickly disappears and the lapse rate again shows a decrease of temperature with increasing height.

In a depression air rises, expands and cools, whereas in an anticyclone the opposite occurs. Air descends and compression and warming take place, resulting in an inversion layer often forming between 3,000 and 5,000ft, *see* Fig. 6.2. When this happens, haze is trapped below the inversion. If the summit of a mountain is above the inversion level, it will be in clear air and above any low cloud, and will be a prime location for sunburn and potential dehydration in the summer.

HUMIDITY

WET BULB EFFECT

The standard method of measuring humidity is based on the difference in readings between an ordinary thermometer (dry bulb), and a thermometer with a damp muslin wick around the bulb (wet bulb). The latent heat of evaporation from the damp muslin wick causes a temperature drop, so the drier the air the greater the difference between the dry and wet bulb.

Exposed flesh responds in a similar way to a wet bulb thermometer. The moisture on the body evaporates, causing a reduction in temperature, with the strength of the wind increasing the rate of evaporation. The resultant cooling is known as the chill factor. The same effect occurs with damp or wet clothing. The combination of low humidity, a strong wind and wet clothes has a considerable cooling effect.

CHILL FACTOR

The chill factor should never be underestimated. It is quite common in 'raw' winter conditions for the chill factor to be mentioned on weather forecasts to emphasise the cooling effect of the wind. For example, with a temperature of 4 °C and a wind speed of 15 knots, the effective temperature is reduced to –3 °C. *See* Fig. 6.3.

Wind speed (knots)	5	10	15	20	25	30
	Effective Temperature					
Temperature °C 8	7	4	2	0	-1	-3
6	5	2	0	-2	-3	-4
4	2	0	-3	-5	-7	-8
2	0	-3	-5	-7	-9	-11
0	-2	-5	-7	-10	-12	-13
-2	-4	-9	-12	-15	-17	-19
-4	-8	-12	-15	-17	-20	-21
-6	-10	-14	-17	-20	-22	-24

Fig. 6.3   Table of the combined effect of temperature and wind.

WIND

In chapter 5, the principles of how and why wind blows relative to weather features were explained. Those principles are applicable to mountains, but the additional effect of topography also needs to be considered. Low-level wind can be assumed to be around a half to two-thirds of the wind at 2,000ft. On that basis alone the wind even half-way up some British mountains can be twice the speed at the bottom. This is a reasonable starting point for an estimation, but there are other factors which can increase the wind speed further.

EXPOSURE

Fig. 6.4 shows a typical air flow over an exposed ridge where the flow is forced over the top. Notice how wind speed increases with height.

Fig. 6.2 explained how a temperature inversion forms in anticyclonic (high-pressure) conditions. If an inversion layer is present just above the top of a ridge, its effect is to increase the flow. The flow just beneath the inversion layer is colder and hence denser than the air above. Consequently the inversion acts as a lid, preventing the air from rising. The result is a funnelling effect of the flow over the top of the ridge, *see* Fig. 6.5.

The one visual clue that might suggest the presence of an inversion is a layer of stratocumulus cloud just above the top of the hills. This is not an infallible guide, but the presence of stratocumulus with a regular base just above the tops of high ground certainly suggests the possibility of a marked increase in wind speed, *see* Fig. 6.6.

FUNNELLING

The funnelling of wind through gaps in a range of hills will also produce a marked increase in wind speed, *see* Fig. 6.7. The wind direction does not always have to be directly across the ridge or through a gap to increase the speed. In Fig. 6.8 the direction is at an angle to the ridge,

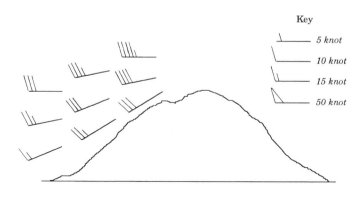

Fig. 6.4   Typical wind flow over a ridge.

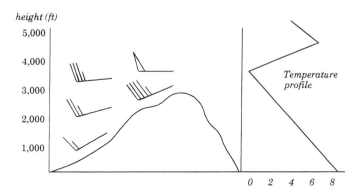

Fig. 6.5   The funnelling effect of an inversion layer.

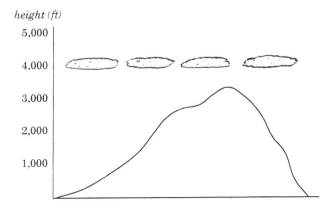

Fig. 6.6 The presence of a layer of stratocumulus cloud just above the top of the ridge may indicate the presence of an inversion layer.

which produces a channelling rather than a funnelling effect, but it still increases the wind speed.

LIGHT WINDS AT DAWN

At night, under clear skies, the air near the ground cools rapidly, forming a temperature inversion. Friction between the cold dense air and the ground increases with the result that the wind near the surface becomes very light or even calm. Around dawn when the inversion is still present, there is often little or no wind in a valley or at low level. Yet even 500–1,000ft higher it would not be uncommon to find a wind of 25 to 30 knots at this time.

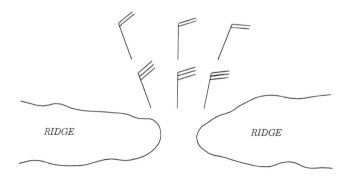

Fig. 6.7 Funnelling between a range of hills will increase wind speed.

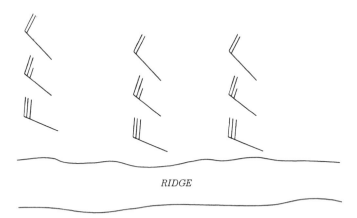

Fig. 6.8 Channelling along a ridge also increases wind speed.

KATABATIC WIND

When there is little or no prevailing wind, a wind can be induced by local effects in the hills and mountains. As the air in contact with the ground cools at night, it becomes more dense and 'slides' down the hillside. The result is a katabatic wind. In general the effect in British mountains is not particularly pronounced, although it does occur. For maximum effect a long gentle snow- or ice-covered slope is required where the flow of air can build up to exceed gale force. The most extreme cases occur in the Antarctic.

ANABATIC WIND

The opposite effect occurs after dawn when the air in contact with the ground warms at the bottom of a valley and starts to rise up the side of a mountain. The result is an anabatic wind. The effect is greatest on south-east slopes facing the Sun in the morning.

CHANGES IN WIND DIRECTION

The expression 'the wind plays tricks in the mountains' is true in so far as topography can influence not only speed but also direction. At any given point the wind can blow in completely the opposite direction to the

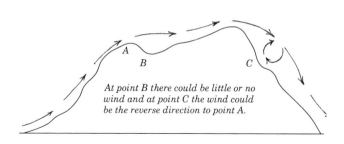

At point B there could be little or no wind and at point C the wind could be the reverse direction to point A.

Fig. 6.9   Changes in wind direction caused by topography.

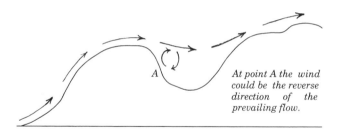

At point A the wind could be the reverse direction of the prevailing flow.

Fig. 6.10   Changes in wind direction over a steep-sided valley.

general flow. Forecasting such changes is impossible, although explaining why a particular directional change occurred is not difficult after the event.

Consider the example given in Fig. 6.9. At point A there is a strong wind blowing from the west, at point B there is virtually no wind at all, yet at point C there is a wind from the opposite direction, a difference of 180 degrees from point A. Fig. 6.10 shows the possible flow over a steep-sided valley. Therefore, with differing topography it is possible to arrive at various combinations of directions and speeds, often lasting no more than a few minutes as the flow fluctuates.

SHELTER FROM THE WIND

There are various reasons why people venture on to hills and mountains, but a time normally comes for most to rest and enjoy the view. It makes sense to find some shelter from the buffeting of the wind, particularly on a cold day. Even if there are no obvious points of shelter in terms of strategically placed rocks, a look at the dips and peaks of the ground in relation to the general direction of the wind may still indicate some sheltered areas.

SEVEN

PRECIPITATION

The term precipitation covers all forms of rain, drizzle, snow and hail. A glance at an isohyet chart (isohyet lines join points of equal rainfall) shows that higher rainfall values coincide with high ground. Since the first requirement for rain is cloud and there is generally more cloud over high ground, this is hardly surprising. Precipitation forms in several different ways, coalescence (water to water), accretion (water to ice), and aggregation (ice to ice).

COALESCENCE

For the formation of water droplets, minute particles are required in the atmosphere for water vapour to condense on to. The most common and efficient are salt particles.

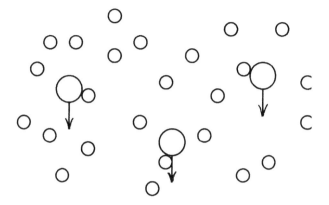

Fig. 7.1 Coalescence. Larger droplets falling through the cloud collide with the smaller droplets. Coalescence takes place, increasing the size of the water droplet.

Once condensation takes place and clouds form, it does not necessarily follow that rain will occur, because obviously there are millions of tiny droplets suspended in a cloud. It is in the presence of rather larger droplets that rain drops are formed by the process of coalescence. The larger drops increase in size as they drift about, 'sweeping up' the smaller droplets. In reality this is a fairly slow and inefficient process for rain formation, except over the sea, coast and mountains.

WEGENER-BERGERON-FINDEISEN PROCESS

Like many of the early ideas on meteorology, the theory for the most efficient method of rain formation was put forward by the Norwegian school of meteorologists. Wegener, Bergeron and Findeisen are now synonymous with, and have given their names to, the process of the growth of raindrops. It is regarded as the process responsible for most rainfall.

Perhaps the most important point to remember is that water droplets can exist as liquid water at very low temperatures (possibly down to −40˚C), providing they are not disturbed. Water droplets at sub-zero temperatures are known as supercooled.

Most clouds are a mixture of supercooled water droplets and ice particles. At critical temperatures (the most efficient temperature is around −12˚C) the supercooled water droplets will evaporate and the water vapour will be deposited on to the ice crystals.

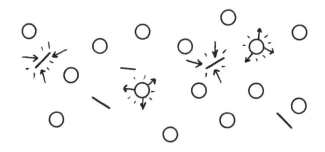

Fig. 7.2   The Wegener–Bergeron–Findeison process. As the supercooled water droplets evaporate water vapour is deposited directly on to the ice crystals.

In other words the ice crystals will grow at the expense of the supercooled water droplets, as in Fig 7.2. This is known as the Wegener–Bergeron–Findeisen process and can produce ice crystals large enough to have a fall speed in only a few minutes.

ACCRETION

Once the ice crystals start to fall they will grow by collision, partly with other ice crystals but principally with supercooled water droplets. As the water droplets are disturbed, they will freeze onto, and increase the size of, the ice crystals. This process is known as accretion, *see* Fig. 7.3 below.

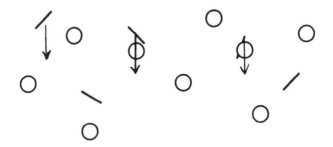

Fig. 7.3   Accretion. As the ice crystals fall through the cloud they 'disturb' the supercooled water droplets. The water droplets then freeze on to the ice crystals.

AGGREGATION

Ice crystals at very low temperatures have a tendency to bounce off each other when they collide. When the temperature is only just below freezing, the ice crystals are more likely to stick together on contact, leading to the formation of snowflakes. This process is known as aggregation. The snowflakes will then either melt as they fall or reach the ground as snow if the air is sufficiently cold.

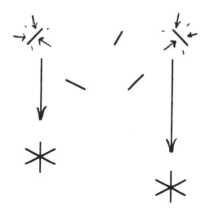

Fig. 7.4 Aggregation. Microscopic ice crystals initially grow by deposition of water vapour onto the crystals. When they are large enough to attain a fall speed, they grow by collision with other ice crystals to form snowflakes. This is an efficient process at temperatures between 0 and −5 °C.

HAIL

Hailstones are associated with cumulonimbus clouds. The initial hailstones are formed from ice crystals (or possibly frozen raindrops) which then grow by various processes, principally accretion. As the hailstones collide with supercooled water droplets, the droplets spread out around the hailstones, increasing their size. The process continues as the hailstones fall through the cloud, sometimes being swept upwards again in the strong updraughts before falling to the ground.

Fig. 7.5   Cross-section through a hailstone. The supercooled water droplets spread out around the hailstone forming layers, in some cases trapping air within the layer.

EIGHT

THUNDERSTORMS

Thunderstorms are normally associated with cumulo-nimbus cloud but very occasionally they can originate from altocumulus castellanus cloud. This is a medium-level cloud with a rather turreted or 'lumpy' appearance.

Recognition of cumulonimbus varies depending on the air mass. In polar maritime air with clear visibility, the clouds are fairly easily recognised. The tops of the cloud tend to stand out clearly, often catching the sunlight. However, with a hazy continental air mass, the definition of the cloud becomes less distinct and cloud identification becomes increasingly difficult. The one occasion when recognition becomes almost impossible is when a cumulonimbus cloud is mixed up (embedded) with other layers of cloud. This can occur in particular along a cold front, when the passage of a front, especially over the high ground, is sometimes accompanied by a thunderstorm. The one common feature of cumulonimbus is that the depth of the cloud and its high water content will inevitably make the sky darken appreciably as the cloud approaches.

Apart from the presence of cumulonimbus cloud, the other obvious sign of an approaching storm is the sound of thunder. Sound travels at approximately 720mph (or 1 mile in 5 seconds), so the time lapse between a flash of lightning and the sound of thunder will give an indication of how far away the storm is. Bearing in mind that lightning can travel sideways for some distance before going to ground, precautions should be taken if there is lightning within 2 miles (10 seconds between flash and bang).

LIGHTNING

The chances of a person being struck by lightning, either directly or indirectly, can be measured in millions to one, and the chance of a lightning strike proving fatal is statistically around one in four. Some people have been struck several times and survived. The body does not retain an electrical charge and the normal methods of resuscitation should be applied if the heart has stopped beating. Being caught out in the open increases the risk of a strike but there are still precautions that can be taken. Most people are aware that it is dangerous to shelter under a lone, prominent tree, which is more likely to attract a strike. Not only is there a danger of a 'side flash' from the tree to a person but there is also the danger of explosive expansion of the moisture in the tree causing injury.

Lightning usually seeks the shortest route to ground, so prime targets are the highest, most prominent points. Pointed objects are the most likely to attract a strike so a pointed peak is a particularly dangerous location, although it does have the effect of offering protection to the surrounding area. On exposed high ground with no available shelter, the best option is to get off any peaks or prominent points, lay aside any metal objects and look for a suitable hollow. The recommended position is to crouch with the head down, feet together, and the hands on either side of the knees or ankles. Lying flat is not recommended because of the danger of a strike nearby, since the length of the body offers resistance to the outward spread effect of the strike along the ground, especially if the ground is wet.

Indications of an imminent strike in the vicinity can occasionally produce rather alarming effects which should be sufficient to alert anyone to the immediate danger. The ground under a storm takes on a positive charge and the effect of a positive electrical charge streaming upwards can make hair stand on end and metal objects start to buzz.

RAINFALL OVER HIGH GROUND

A glance at a rainfall map shows that the areas of greatest rainfall coincide with the high ground. This is due to a number of factors. As we have already seen, the effect of uplift over the hills enhances the formation of convective cloud. This can lead to cumulonimbus and cumulus of sufficient depth to produce frequent showers. In a moist flow over mountains, the uplift results in extensive low cloud formation. Any rain falling from higher level cloud is increased by coalescence as it falls through the low cloud. This is known as the 'seeder-feeder' process and

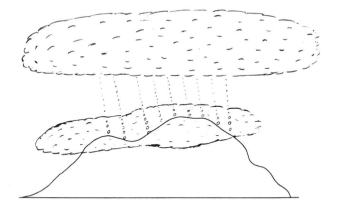

Fig. 8.1   The 'seeder-feeder' process. The raindrops increase in size as they fall through the cloud at lower level.

the 'washed out' droplets are the feeder part. The effect is enhanced in a strong low-level flow, particularly when associated with a slow moving front. It becomes even more pronounced at the head of a valley where the wind is funnelled uphill, producing a marked change in rainfall amounts over quite a short distance.

NINE

WEATHER FORECASTS

Since the introduction of operational computers for weather forecasting in the early 1960s, the standard has steadily improved. The concept of producing forecasts mathematically (numerical forecasts) is by no means a new idea. The principle was set out around 1920 by an early meteorologist, Lewis Fry Richardson. At that time the magnitude of making the necessary calculations manually took so long that the forecast became an irrelevance. It was not until computers were able to cope with high speed 'number-crunching' that producing forecasts numerically became a practical reality. There is still a role to play for the human forecaster in interpretation, and also 'fine tuning' in the short term, but the computer forecast is now an essential part of the forecast procedure.

It is inadvisable to set out on to the mountains of the British Isles without a good idea of the current and expected weather conditions. Forecasts for the mountains and high ground are now readily available on computer and mobile phones.

UNITS OF MEASUREMENT

Units of measurement used in meteorology tend to be a mixture of metric and imperial, for example visibility distances are measured in metres and kilometres yet cloud heights are measured in feet. It would be confusing to talk of cloud with a base 2,500ft covering a 1,000m mountain. Hence all heights, both cloud and mountains, are referred to in feet.

Temperatures have always been something of a hotchpotch in forecasts, with the terms Fahrenheit, Centigrade and Celsius all being used at various times. For many years the standard unit in British forecasts was Fahrenheit and indeed many people still refer to temperatures on a hot day as being 'in the eighties'. However, the standard unit now in use is Celsius, the international unit of temperature measurement, and the unit used in forecasts. (Note that Celsius is the same as Centigrade.)

Wind speeds are generally measured in knots although the speeds in most forecasts are given in miles per hour. (Just to complicate the situation some countries measure wind speed in metres per second!) The measurement used in this book is knots or miles per hour (mph) where appropriate for scale..

USEFUL CONVERSION FACTORS

Length/height   1 metre   = 3.28084 feet
                 1 kilometre = 0.62137 statute miles

Speed   1 knot   = 1.152 miles per hour

Temperature

°C	°F	°C	°F	°C	°F	°C	°F	°C	°F	°C	°F
–20	–04	–10	14	00	32	10	50	20	68	30	86
–19	–02	–09	16	01	34	11	52	21	70	31	88
–18	00	–08	18	02	36	12	54	22	72	32	90
–17	01	–07	19	03	37	13	55	23	73	33	91
–16	03	–06	21	04	39	14	57	24	75	34	93
–15	05	–05	23	05	41	15	59	25	77	35	95
–14	07	–04	25	06	43	16	61	26	79	36	97
–13	09	–03	27	07	45	17	63	27	81	37	99
–12	10	–02	28	08	46	18	64	28	82	38	100
–11	12	–01	30	09	48	19	66	29	84	39	102

THE BEAUFORT SCALE

The traditional way to estimate the wind speed is by using the Beaufort scale, which was compiled by Admiral Sir Francis Beaufort in the early part of the nineteenth century. It was originally meant for use at sea, giving descriptions of the sea state appropriate to a range of wind speeds. Subsequently it was adapted for observers on land, but has limited use in the mountain environment due to the absence of trees, on which many of the observations are based. Even so, it is still worth being aware of the descriptive speed terms, 'fresh to strong' etc.

It might be possible to compile a version for the mountain environment with reference to the movement of lying snow by the wind, or the difficulty of walking in the higher ranges of the scale. There is obviously a point, for example, when the strength of the wind makes walking tiring, and a point at which it is difficult to stand upright. However, at the present time no such scale exists.

FORCE	DESCRIPTIVE TERM	SPECIFICATION
0	Calm	Smoke rises vertically.
1	Light air	Direction of wind shown by smoke drift, but not by wind vane.
2	Light breeze	Wind felt on face; leaves rustle; ordinary vanes moved by wind.
3	Gentle breeze	Leaves and small twigs in constant motion; wind extends light flag.
4	Moderate breeze	Raises dust and loose paper; small branches are moved.
5	Fresh breeze	Small trees in leaf begin to sway.
6	Strong breeze	Large branches in motion; whistling heard in telegraph wire; umbrellas used with difficulty.
7	Near gale	Whole trees in motion; inconvenience felt when walking against the wind.
8	Gale	Breaks twigs off trees; generally impedes progress.
9	Strong gale	Slight structural damage (chimney pots and slates removed).
10	Storm	Seldom experienced inland; trees uprooted; considerable structural damage occurs.
11	Violent storm	Very rarely experienced; accompanied by widespread damage.

GLOSSARY OF TERMS

Air mass	Air with similar characteristics in terms of temperature and humidity.
Anabatic wind	An upslope wind, induced by local heating.
Anemometer	Instrument for measuring wind speed and direction.
Anticyclone	A region of high pressure. Sometimes referred to as a 'high'.
Backing	A shift of wind direction in an anti-clockwise direction.
Barometer	Instrument for measuring atmospheric pressure.
Buys Ballot's law	An important meteorological law which states that with one's back to the wind the low pressure will always be on the left in the northern hemisphere and on the right in the southern hemisphere.
Chill factor	The enhanced cooling effect of the wind.
Condensation	The process of water vapour condensing to form liquid water.
Convection	The process by which warmer air rises and cooler air sinks.
Convective cloud	Cloud, usually cumulus and cumulonimbus, formed when air is forced to rise through heating, and then cools and condensation occurs.

Coriolis force	The apparent deflection of air due to the Earth's rotation. The deflection is to the right in the northern hemisphere and to the left in the southern hemisphere.
Cyclone	An area of low pressure. Normally referred to as a 'low' or depression in the temperate latitudes.
Depression	*See* Cyclone.
Dew point	Temperature at which condensation will form when air is cooled.
Drizzle	Small drops of liquid precipitation falling from layer cloud.
Evaporation	The process by which water (liquid) becomes water vapour (gas).
Fog	The term used when the visibility is less than 1,000m, caused by the suspension of water droplets in the air.
Front	The division between two air masses. A warm front refers to warm air replacing cold air, and a cold front refers to cold air replacing warm air.
Geostrophic wind	The balanced air flow between the pressure gradient force and the Coriolis force. The approximate wind at 2,000ft.
High	*See* Anticyclone.
Inversion	The condition in which the temperature increases with height in contrast to the normal decrease.
Isobar	Line on a weather chart joining points of equal pressure.
Isohyet	Line on a weather chart joining points of equal rainfall values.

Jet stream	A high level 'ribbon' of fast flowing air.
Katabatic wind	A wind blowing down a slope, caused by nocturnal or glacial cooling.
Lapse rate	The rate of change of temperature with height.
Low	*See* Cyclone.
Occlusion	An amalgamation of a warm and cold front when the warm sector has been lifted off the surface.
Pressure gradient force	The force caused by the pressure differential between an area of high and low pressure.
Rain	Liquid precipitation of water droplets of size greater than 0.5mm.
Showers	Precipitation, either liquid or solid, falling from convective cloud.
Sleet	A mixture of rain and snow, although the term is often used to describe wet snow that melts on landing.
Stratosphere	The layer in the atmosphere above the troposphere.
Thermals	Columns of rising air induced by heating.
Tropopause	The boundary between the troposphere and stratosphere.
Troposphere	The lowest layer of the atmosphere extending from the Earth's surface to approximately 12km. This is the layer in which clouds and weather occur.
Trough	An extension of an area of low pressure; often associated with a line of cloud and possibly showers.
Veering	A shift of wind direction in a clockwise direction.

| Warm sector | The region following a warm front and ahead of a cold front. |
| Wet bulb | A thermometer with a damp muslin wick around the bulb. The difference in readings between an ordinary thermometer and a wet bulb thermometer indicates the humidity. |

FURTHER READING

Atkinson, Professor B.W. and Gadd, Dr Alan, *A Modern Guide to Weather Forecasting* (Mitchell Beazley, 1986)

Langmuir, Eric, *Mountaincraft and Leadership* (The Scottish Sports Council and the Mountain Leadership Training Board, 1984)

Pedgley, Dave, *Mountain Weather* (Cicerone Press, 1979)

File, Dick, *Weather Facts* (Oxford University Press, 1990)

INDEX